strangers

strangers

poems

rob taylor

BIBLIOASIS

WINDSOR, ON

FIRST EDITION

Library and Archives Canada Cataloguing in Publication

Title: Strangers : poems / Rob Taylor.
Names: Taylor, Rob, 1983- author.
Description: Poems.
Identifiers: Canadiana (print) 2021012248X | Canadiana (ebook) 20210122501 | ISBN 9781771964197
 (softcover) | ISBN 9781771964203 (ebook)
Classification: LCC PS8639.A9555 S77 2021 | DDC C811/.6—dc23

Edited by Luke Hathaway
Copyedited by Emily Donaldson
Text and cover designed by Christina Angeli

Published with the generous assistance of the Canada Council for the Arts, which last year invested $153 million to bring the arts to Canadians throughout the country, and the financial support of the Government of Canada. Biblioasis also acknowledges the support of the Ontario Arts Council (OAC), an agency of the Government of Ontario, which last year funded 1,709 individual artists and 1,078 organizations in 204 communities across Ontario, for a total of $52.1 million, and the contribution of the Government of Ontario through the Ontario Book Publishing Tax Credit and Ontario Creates.

PRINTED AND BOUND IN CANADA

For Jim Sr., Jim Jr. and Jon

For we are who we are, and more, all that is ridden within us in the same way our fathers are not our fathers but someone else's inconsolable sons

— Chris Banks

Contents

"But we are different," she said. "I would have us exactly the same."

"You do not mean that."

"Yes I do. I do. That is a thing I had to tell thee."

"You do not mean that."

"Perhaps I do not," she said speaking softly with her lips against his shoulder. "But I wished to say it."

— Maria to Robert,
For Whom The Bell Tolls

Strangers

At three, on vacation, my mother and I alone
on an aerial tour (two seats, no exceptions),
my father waving until he was very small
then unfolding the paper from under his armpit,
I wept with the depth of the assured—
the Ruahine Range irrelevant below.

My mother asked, coddled, pleaded.
The pilot offered ridiculous faces,
an early return. Only in the sight
of my father, rising from a bench beside
the helipad, hand raised again in greeting,
was my world, pulled apart, reassembled.

Nine years later his hand, warm,
was thirty minutes later cold. I watched
him wheeled away. I held his ashes
and wondered where to put them.
And I waited for his return.
I wait still, whatever sense it makes.

Alright, okay, we do not live forever. Our works
are lost and are not found. There is no consolation.
But, Elise, I read your poems today.
Each rose and greeted me as if everything
was normal, as if my return had been expected.
And in this act I saw my father.

It makes no sense. You would be strangers
if not for this. But I saw him, Elise.
He was your poems.
He was waving and becoming larger.

You ask me about my mother

so I tell you how she slammed
the trunk of our Toyota on my neck
when I was three and wandering
and she was in a rush for groceries.
No harm was done, I say, and so you laugh,
and I laugh, as does my mom
each time she hears me tell my story
which isn't mine, of course, but hers—
my brain back then a roil of loose ends,
a squall within which stories wouldn't last
unless she lashed them there: the scene,
the thud and wail, the nightmare snap
that might have been, the unexpected ways
that terror rises from its resting place
beneath. All these she offered me,
wrapped within her story and her laugh,
the laugh which smoothed the knots
and fused the sea
inside me.

Smoothing the Holy Surfaces

One winter, two a.m., his doctor's
bad prescription setting in,
my dad went into shock—
my mom ten-minute-tumbled
his six-two, two-fifty tremble to the car,
the windshield scraped, ignition on,
before she caught a vision of my cherub's face
tucked above my covers.

She scooped me up too quickly, swung
around towards the car, her ears
astounded by the sound as cherub-skull
thwacked doorframe. Then came the blood.
Then the startled screams from both our mouths,
the comic shuffle through sliding doors,
husband hooked on one arm,
jittering akimbo, son slung in the other,
an ornate fountain spurting purple
beneath fluorescent ER lights.

My head stitched up and all of us
in bed before sunrise, death's
nearest pass (despite their fears)
had come as we careened our way downhill
in our clown car of misfortune,
my mother in the driver's seat,
her right hand placing pressure on my skull,
her left gripped hard upon the wheel—
the story she now laughs about at parties
piling up around her like the snow
that fell that night, silently
and everywhere.

That Scar

Fourteen, with hollow, aching limbs
I fed my fingers past empty serving bowls
and plucked a cube of melon from my mother's plate,
her fork cascading down to catch
my knuckle mid-retreat.

Had I been ten or twenty,
had my father been alive,
some innocence or indifference
would have gotten in the way
(civility and all its cobbled barricades).

Instead, that day, she dug down
on the clenched crown of my fist
until the tines began to puddle blood
and our brunch guests' laughter
clotted to a glottal stop.

Our laughter lasted on—
bewildered, joyful, barely seamed
with spite—though I let go.
Eventually I must have
let the damn thing go.

Lunch

We snap out our chopsticks and talk about the weather. After a lull I start in about the Lake Vostok project in Antarctica and how it took them over twenty years to drill down to the surface of the lake, four thousand metres under the ice. That's interesting, she says. Then the waiter arrives with our food. She mangles her California roll and I burn the roof of my mouth on my deep-fried tofu. Eventually she lays her chopsticks down across her bento box and tells me that her friend's doing better, though the cancer is still killing her. She's so skinny now but she bought herself a new wardrobe and can drive her car, so it's not all that bad yet. That's good to hear, I say. The lake is almost as large as Lake Ontario, I add, and it's been trapped under ice for fifteen million years. Then we both say one or two things and somehow we end up talking about her parents, how her mom's folks hated her father so much that he packed up the family and moved north to the mining town just to get away from that mess. The waiter comes around again with the green tea. Neither of us wants more, but we smile politely as he pours. Your dad would have liked the Lake Vostok project, I say. They set a record by drilling the world's deepest ice core. That's something, she says. The waiter brings the bill and she takes it before I get the chance. When he returns with the change it's an awkward amount so I chip in a dollar for the tip. They fill the borehole with Freon and kerosene so it doesn't freeze between drillings, almost sixty tons of the stuff so far. That doesn't sound good, she says. No, I say, but they don't think it will contaminate the lake because as soon as they break the surface, water will rush up the borehole and freeze, sealing out the chemicals. Well I hope so, she says, pulling on her jacket. On our way out we pass a table with a mother and three kids. All the kids have sticky rice in their hair or on their face but none of the four seems to mind. You should write a poem about that, she says. She's never said anything like it before. About what, I ask. But she can't hear me over the street noise and has already moved on to something else.

Speak When Illuminated

I lie in bed, await three knocks from my parents' side
of our adjoining wall, one each for *I, love,* and *you*—
then I reply, with one more added on for too.
And only then we sleep.

I dream I'm in an elevator: an adult, poet,
stubble-cheeked. My father dead, expectedly.
My mother married once again and happy.
My own wife in our home, expectant.
Then the elevator sticks.

I root my fingers in the door. It doesn't give.
I press the button, panic-red, attempting to call out—
to whom? Some maintenance guy? A telecom employee
in Chennai? *Speak When Illuminated*
reads the sign that doesn't light.

To myself, I realize, my mind half waking
from the dream. I am my only rescue.
I stare into the bulb to make it shine.
My wife is out there waiting; my manuscripts
and friends. My mother and my father just outside.
Yes, even him.

My waking mind insists it cannot be. He's too old
to have lasted out these years. No, he's just behind
the wall, I say into myself. I'll show you now.
I knock three times upon the metal door.
Four knocks ring back.

My waking mind falls silent, yields the floor.
I am not a child anymore.

A Normal Day

Rain. The sound of it on the roof. A song on the radio
I'll almost remember tomorrow. Just enough light
to write by. A lamp I know I should switch on.
Soda crackers. Hot water with lemon. Dishes in the sink,
few enough I can put them off a while. In the afternoon
I'll call my mother and we'll talk about nothing,
the weather. I'll ask if it's raining there and she'll say yes.
We'll share some news about family or football,
and maybe reminisce a bit: my childhood, my father,
her life before us both. But mostly the rain,
which will lighten and finally stop around dinner
while my wife and I are filling the house with our talk
so we will not notice the change until hours later,
sitting in bed. One of us will lower their book
and mention it in passing. Or maybe
it will still be raining then, so we'll say nothing
and in the morning we won't be certain
if it ever stopped, or when it did
and when it started up again.

Love, fidelity, etc.

I do not wear you
when I shower, when I sleep,

when playing sports or making things,
my knuckles thick in dirt or grease,

though I wear you now on the hand
behind my head, which tilts it to the page.

Remember when I lost you
those six months beneath the driver's seat?

You must have hidden in my pocket—
the one inside the other—

and when I wriggled out the keys
you ventured too.

Folks think you *represent*
but we both know you're

up there in the darkness of my hair
or, one time, waiting in the car.

When I rediscovered you
we were both prodigals' fathers

grieving our sons,
though it was my hand, of course,

reached out in welcome,
my mouth that rushed the story to my wife.

Yes, you arrived with my marriage.
You'll go at the end, off to some necklace or pouch

or you'll linger years in the earth
until all you encircle is earth

and a scavenger prospects you up,
as I did, from the muck.

It wasn't much. I was in the field.
I knelt. My hands were bare.

The bucket is blue and deep
and brims with cool water

My wife this early evening
is the sound of splashing water.
From time to time she lifts the cup
up high enough above the concrete
shower wall to turn into a hand,
a wrist, a lathered arm. She tips
the cup and spills back out of sight.
It's then I notice, finally, the clouds
that journey slow above, the breeze
that drives them on, that dips down
every night and drives her, too, to dry
and dress and navigate the distance
between her sound of splashing water
and myself, a path I notice now
is mapped with dirt and grass and brush
and fading light and molecules.
Molecules! My god! And then
the hand, the wrist, the arm
rise up, obliterate them all.

Aubade

I slip in bed beside you
always long asleep and still
and yet some nights
from that dark deep
you turn, reach out
and set one hand upon my chest
or roll yourself against my side
and rest there a few breaths
no more than that, no words
then back and deep and gone
and as we rise and dress
we do not think to speak of it
as once we might have tried—
not at the start
though not long after that
we would have laughed
and lifted praise
to love and what we'd made of it
but now I simply hold you there
a moment in the dark
each of us unsure or dreaming
and words an ancient faith
a fate we long before
abandoned to the light.

Weather in Dublin

The night Heaney died it rained so hard in Vancouver
the gutters clogged, flooding the streets. In all our years
in the city we'd never seen rain like it. We shouted as much
to our neighbours, who were at their windows, and they nodded
and laughed and agreed. We went down to the street, barefoot
with umbrellas, and danced like Gene Kelly and Debbie Reynolds.

The night Heaney died an old woman two buildings over
raced out in a rain slicker, boots and rubber gloves, and worked
with a broom at the storm drains. She hauled up leaves and feathers
and plastic containers and—the wet centre bottomless—
a rock the size of two fists. We watched as water rose up,
breached the curb, rushed over lawns and flower beds,
sloshed against apartment blocks. Humiliated, we stooped
beside her and lowered our hands into the swirling dark.

The night Heaney died it was morning in Dublin,
so what am I going on about? It was thirteen degrees
and partly cloudy. Visibility good, wind from the southwest.
The light that leaned through the window was bright enough
and soft, I imagine, like the light that greeted us this morning
when we woke and learned the news.

Under our window, a clean rasping sound.
Our neighbours have made their way outside.
They are gathering up the scattered heads of flowers
and talking to each other. One has a rake, another a clear
plastic bag. A third is calling around about water damage.
Two are distributing paper cups full of coffee
and the rest are drinking from them. We call out and wave.
We will remember this morning forever, I am almost sorry to say.

late summer walk
slanting my father's Issa
to catch streetlight

Ultrasound

—with lines from Rainer Maria Rilke

We can hardly hint at you
so tomorrow we'll send
the restless Doppler out
and hope to find inside
an awareness *our senses
cannot fathom this night*,
like your skull peeling back
to grey matter—your life
and the death inside it,
squirming from the camera.

I cannot uncouple them
even now. *So be the meaning
of their strange encounter.*
Your death and the life
inside it. All of us
gathered in the hospital
to marvel *at their crossing*—
the dark screen before
and after and all around
you, *the radiant centre.*

The Future

Reading a poem about the dead, I realize
that for the first time in my life I am far from them,
which means, of course, that they are very close
in the direction I'm not looking.

Death, like a fine muslin you wrapped
every part of me—my eyes, my mouth.
Whenever I believed I'd escaped, I'd only turned,
tightened or loosened your grip—

until today, when I cannot feel you,
not even tangled at my feet.
When I whip around
I can almost see them:
my father, my son, together.

The future behind me.
Now the past.

Colic

Eventually it's not all darkness.
The outline of my desk. Dull shapes
of bassinet and bookshelf.
He's asleep but must go deeper.
Each sway I hush, and count
the hushes. One hundred more.
My pupils wide enough to welcome
a seam of streetlight through the blinds.
Your painting of the moon
a smudge of light on canvas.
The picture of my father, two decades
dead, the same. Our wedding photo
now your dress' ghost form, dipped,
my arm a black band holding it aloft.
A magic trick. We planned for this
but we did not plan for this. Fifty more
and then perhaps two hours' sleep.
Now his forehead, cheeks, a haze of legs
frogged in my arm. I can't see his eyes
within their hollows, but I would see the white.
I can see his open lips, but not the bottom
of the well, that hole that swallows villages.
Soon enough I will see everything.
Okay. Okay. One hundred more. I can't see
my body but I feel it. I never hated him.
That was just an ache. It's four a.m.
and you're asleep in the next room
and the light is making its way to me,
gray and glowing and becoming our son.

Transatlantic

The yellow tail
of a train
trailing sulphur
split the track
in two.

I have come
from visiting
my brother,
disease piled
snug in him
like cargo
in a transatlantic
hold.

At the edge
of my vision
a switch
where the train
paused a moment,
powder
pyramiding
beneath it.

"You're going
to make it," I'd said,
and whatever
that meant,
I'd meant it.

November, Six a.m.

Colic ragged in my son's throat, I rolled
him, raging alarm clock, block by block
through our neighbours' Fabergé dreams.

The sparrow we found was far from dead,
some minor gouges in its neck, its contract killers
driven back like Noriega from the Holy See.

I sidled up and waited for the dun
and orange lump to hobble into flight.
I rocked my child back and forth.

The songbird nuzzled the softened silver fringe
of some high-end condo's lawn—one eye on me, its legs
snap-thin, the whole thing occupied with breath.

The crows bobbed nearby, sleek
and weaponized. My baby cried and cried,
and even in that fog I felt the metaphor align.

Minutes passed. Eyes strained through
venetian blinds. Eventually my first-born slept.
The sparrow didn't rise.

I scooped it up and walked the six blocks home.
Its head—black eye and beak—locked stiff,
the rest alive against my glove.

I set it in some brush and scanned the skies.
The sky.
Then I pushed the two of us inside.

The Jockey of Artemision

A child still and always, eyes
and mouth, once bone, now bowls
hollowed those millennia below
the waves, no reins to guide the horse
gigantic underneath his thighs.
All he clings to—all he sees
and speaks of now—is time
and what it takes and what,
a while, it leaves behind.

My son, strapped to my chest,
reaches for the sculpture
as he strains for everything these days.
No, I say. He shrinks back, pauses, tries
again. The docents laugh and coo,
relaxed, though we are all aware
in time he'll reach, race through and past.
That future boy, beyond our grasp,
relentless, reinless, silent, blind.

One Lie

Intelligence is nothing. Money is nothing.
Power, comfort, independence, protection
are nothing. Strength is nothing. Confidence,
talent, assurance are nothing. Looks are nothing.
The colour of your eyes is nothing. The length
of your fingers, the swell of your belly: nothing.
Your eyelashes are nothing but eyelashes. Your teeth
are only a pain in the mouth. Your skin is brand new
every month. The cries you make and the cries
we make rock in the air until they are nothing.
Quiet is the air relaxing its arms. Sleep is joy
and practice, how you learn to let things come.
Milk is but one of milk's many forms. Desire's
a chicken and death's an egg. The heart's
an organ, compassion's an engine, solidarity
is all in the hands. Luck is nothing. Glory is nothing.
Wisdom is restless. Success and failure
are the horn and its unicorn. History is the air
entering and exiting your lungs. Art is an emptying,
arrogance pursed lips, vanity a mirror
in someone else's house. Kindness is the roots
that ruin lawn mowers. Courage is a madman
guessing right. Sanity is what you make of it.
Addiction is waves on the beach. Fear travels
in packs. Grief drags its tail. The rained-on page
stiffens but is not the same. Fire is the end
greeting the beginning. Fate is nothing. Loss is nothing.
Love is not everything, no, I am sorry to say.

Krakatoa

On the other side of the world
my brother is dying.
Not one sound can be heard
from the other side of the world,
not even an island unfurled—
so what's the point in crying?
From the other side of the word
brother, my brother, I'm trying.

3 M

Dust-tufted thimbles,
industrial orange puffs
picked ragged from finger-tipped
trip upon trip cockroached snug
beneath my brain's awning.

I roll the foam thin, slip it in.
The max-volume monitor
that dull-roars the void
now a whisper, the boy
in the bugged room yawning,

his mind flicking to colour.
I draw the blinds, close my eyes,
pray in my sprawling
for an hour tucked tight
to the source of my longing—

then his waking moan
(that monk's hum, that sine wave,
that high-alpine slide)
can crash through these gates
like a dawning.

What Wisdom's in Wisdom Recorded?

It is a silver morning like any other.

—Mary Oliver

"One day I won't be a poet," says the poet,
wind knotted in an oak's pocket
beside the flayed arbutus.

Our son's a torture. He won't rest.
We ask him what a wave says and too fast
his crash falters back to the shell of its birth.

Somewhere a deer in a clearing
seeks a human eye.
I haven't slept well in over a year.

Mary, tell me more of your planet.
Of wonder I am welcoming, of negativity
more than capable.

The houses that line the Pacific
are thin and near invincible.
Gabled, with festive trim, they rattle.

How warm, how pliable,
our common aloneness,
our asking and giving in the dark.

Mary, our mornings are mornings.
Our son's sounds vanish with each.
Less and less is summoned from the bed.

Wake me when you wake yourself
I scrawl and stick
to the bathroom mirror.

My flesh is raw, like any other's, and smooth.
So when the poet ends the poem
I believe them.

At Roblin Lake

As the Dream Holds the Real

When you cross the doorway you feel them
when you cross the places they've been

—Al Purdy

Two a.m., naked and whipped
by a slow-drowning winter
I pad out a log, place it
shuddering in so the baby
won't freeze, no cry as my shin
welcomes some edge of the new
old world at Roblin, no shout
as the almost-not orange
shifts shadow to mouse
then rain-barrel squirrel
then pilgrim goggling glass
and not till I'm safe
siphoning heat from my slow-
burning wife, does the log
with a generous crack
unfurl its dormant proportions.

Survival

Be Alarmed!

−*Carbon Monoxide Public Safety Billboard,*
Belleville, Ontario

Red-eyed anachronism huffing between hutches.
My son asleep in an adjacent room. Ten minutes
till he's scheduled to wake. The oven hums,
fire hisses its demands, hot water tank clicks off
then on. The snow, unwelcomed, comes and comes.
I double check—the goddamn thing's a pest deterrent,
its screams beyond our human range. The traps
we set are subtler than when coal oil lamps
lit this room and roadkill rabbit hit the menu.
Now teapots cluster under glass. Each life is twinned—
what happens and what could. I rush and open wide
the door, imagine poison pouring out.
Snow blusters in the entry. Five minutes,
then I'll lift him warm into the day.
One arm around my neck, he'll stretch and sigh.
Later I will mop the melt, head down,
as someone else's story masses silently outside.

Untitled

Spring, the laggard, stumbled in
so I read the week-old *Globe* instead
as the fire's five-day ash grew cold.
The astronomers have told us
of a new black hole
seventeen billion suns in size
that's squatting in some sparse
galaxy, shattering established
size-to-fuel ratios. I hovered
my hand over the coals—*good enough*—
then went to work, careful
with the long-necked shovel, but ash
still billowed up, coated hands
and face and scalp, the facets
of the room. And yes of course
I thought of Purdy's piled blood
and my father's ashes, both
back in Vancouver—
the blood now some novel
atomic arrangement, some dirt
or flower; the ashes in their urn
in my mother's closest, twenty-two years
awaiting transformation. Hours passed,
then Spring hitched back to Toronto.
I lit a match and seared straight through
the black heart of the artist's rendering.
Now it's morning. My wife and son
are still asleep. The bedroom's cold.
Ash is on my pillow, seventeen billion
black suns are trash-compacting the sky
and I'm hungrier than I've been in years.
But instead of getting up, I'm writing a poem.
Lord, I would swallow this paper.
I would burn it.
My heavenly father, give me a sign.

The Point

Look what a few people doing,
and a few more talking, can accomplish—
turn some scrap of land hallowed.

Ice leapt from the lake today
and gathered in the brambles,
though it was water until it landed.

It hung in icicles, bubbled
on the shore, slanted
everything it touched.

When I stepped on it, I broke through,
though for a moment it held me there
an inch above the earth.

Fire Pit

If you need to talk you light a fire
then I stop and come outside
and we set aside at least an hour
to watch the wood unwind
until its heat becomes our thoughts
against the night, its flames
one another's faces.

Our son is nearly nine months old.
He rages through his days,
hell-bent to crawl. Slips backward
under couches, tables—howls
from the bottoms of those wells.
Some mornings, before he cries out
from his crib, we hear him
rocking back and forth on palms
and knees, practising escape.

Seventeen years together
without a fire pit. All those hours.
Now how a silent minute glows.
I lower him exhausted into sleep.
You angle wood into a tower.
No moon tonight, the lake and trees
interlocking fingers.
The shadow of your body—
cradle of our self-cradling son—
bends and sparks *hello*,
that pin of light inside the letting go.

County Roads

Driving to deepen your sleep, as my stepfather
does to feel awake against Coquihalla winds. Driving
whatever direction, each stop a meeting place
of four empty fields huddled against the evening.
This morning, your mother holding you at the front door,
you waved goodbye to me—stretched four fingers out
then to your palm. It was your first word,
that opening and closing. I responded in kind
and the three of us stayed there, amazed, passing goodbyes
back and forth until you looked away. Later,
we watched a flock of terns circle a flooded field, a storm's
gray gauze only one hill over and whipping its way.
You tucked your head against my chest, your eyes following
the reeling white birds. Now I take another corner,
rattle through an ambush of potholes. You don't stir.
It's the motion, I know. The speed and turns and vibrations.
And also, I tell myself, your being just the right distance
from me. Facing the rear windshield, the night curling past,
curving backward, rewinding almost, and me
always a foot behind you, a foot ahead of you,
unzipping and zipping the darkness around us, the road
endless, your dreams buzzing like morning glories, turning,
stretching, folding, opening, closing, driving, driving.

Interruption

O, what a panic's in thy breastie!

—Robbie Burns

The first was dead, a dull dishwater fog
nudging my wife's hand. Her shock
shot our family into the day. The second
I scooped and sealed in a yogurt cup,
left it to ferry itself, afloat on its own CO_2.
Now mice are everywhere:
plastered in tire treads; upturned
under brambles; desiccating among
gutter leaves, no telling twig from tail.
Like to a newly taught word we've been tuned.

Cardboard and duct tape and sheeting and screws.
Tip traps and neck-snaps and a chemical map
marking off the house's hutched corners—
terrible, tolerable only until the baby crawls.
Why hasn't he yet? Has Hanta already set in,
our surfaces leathered with piss? We scrub
at the play mats, scour our dreams,
and listen, each evening, as the dead
filibuster behind the great baseboard,
unwilling to share what they've seen.

I'd placed it, one hour, outside.
My wife had arrived, agreed, then wept
there in Purdy's old kitchen, aglow beneath
its banished amber bulbs. What could I do?
Five farmers' fields, then I plopped it
lolling like my baby drunk and flooded
from a heady feed. How close had it been?
That fabled in-between of made-for-TV movies?
Breathe, I said. *That's what almost did me in*,
its eyes replied. Then its helpless lungs obliged.

Last Embers

no one knows / whether they represent life or death

—Louise Glück

Pot after pot we pour upon them, back and forth
from the kitchen sink, laughing at your mid-sentence
pause delivering Purdy's line—"during the fall
plowing a man"—the embers going as poems go
as we go barefoot back and forth across the grass,
the house blazing behind sliding glass, but really
just waiting and warm, the baby asleep further inside,
maybe waking as the glass opens and closes, feeling
the air shift, smelling embers, tasting smoke,
hearing his parents' laughter and knowing then
that the night, too, requires attendance
and sensing a jealousy gather faintly around him,
too faintly, then easily shaking its hold.

Last Mouse

One more for the season, for the nose,
hidden on a high shelf. Fur lifted, a grey puff,
a blanket of self pulled over itself. I toss the cup's
contents outside, a bead in the brambles,
the fur a living thing skittering up.

My mother's visiting. She's inside
washing the cup, all the cups
the mouse might have turned up in.
She's come cross-country
for a few days with her grandson (and us).

The four of us sit on the couch,
the boy on her lap, the three of them
playing. I slouch my head to my mother's
shoulder, close my eyes, and listen
as my life lifts off around me.

Cemetery

Al, it's five p.m. and my son is still in his pajamas.
He's strapped to me as together we water your flowers.

I doubt you'd have liked me. I don't drink.
I make nice. I stunt my opinions.

My son pulls my pen to his mouth
and chews it awhile.

I watch, contented, as some magnificent
stretch of my poem disappears.

I don't think you'd approve.
Still, I'm glad I'm here with you today.

My student was fifteen, and died last night
in her sleep in Vancouver.

Every thing, by definition, has edges.
I'm not here to ask you to pass on a message.

If we'd met you wouldn't have let me crash one night
in the loft. Now I've slept two months in your bed.

My pen, restored, sputters through my son's drool.
I'll be quick, while it lasts.

Thank you, Al, for the A-frame, the poems,
this anchor you dropped by the millpond.

For ferrying nothing, not one blooming word,
with you across its black eye.

ink on paper—
swatting mosquitoes
with my father's Issa

Voices

Would I still love the creek if I lasted forever?

—Jim Harrison

In my dream
my brother is dying
again. Again, the quiet.
Out of it he says
look at this
and he means
all of us
gathered together
as we gathered
for our father
twenty years before—
less a lie
than a beautiful dream
inside the dream.

And somewhere in there
I know of course
that I am all of us,
my brother, myself,
every member
of our family
living and dead.
I am glad my brother says
in my weakest voice,
tears in my eyes,
that you are here.
And he means all of us,
Jim, even you
so far away in love.

The Artist

The bird sings. Its feathers shine.

—Wallace Stevens

My son, too young, toddles to the two-
button remote: one to move the T-rex
forward, one to shake its skull and summon up
its patent-pending roar. He roars himself,
defiant, then presses button two
and knows, or seems to know, the noise
arises from his throat and fingers, nowhere else,
so isn't shocked when it arrives
but once the sound has journeyed
thoroughly inside, wide-eyed
he steps back once or twice
where buffer-loved and terror-blind
he lurches his fear forward one more time
and jabs and jabs the jagged jaws alive.

The Long Goodbye

As with water once the stone's dropped in,

a time-lapse spider looping web, a Doppler

blob of cumulonimbus gathering deep

in the Pacific, it's possible to mark

the moment *there* or *there* or *there*. You'll die

and I'll circle when and where the dying

started, shift the timeline back and forth

like a napkin worried in my lap—a distraction

for my hands amidst the mouths. You'll die

and I'll sense when I'd had my chance

and when it passed. Maybe last week

with your doctor's voice or some time

in those six years when I thought your diagnosis

was just another thing that comes with age

or when you had your kids or went away to college—

until one day I'll hurl the lasso all the way to birth

and sense with useless shock the useless fact that one

or one more call would not have been enough.

You'll die, the rain will come, some fly will dawdle by,

the pebble that you held will fall. You'll die

and I'll mark the spot both at the centre and the edge,

your face so clear it's lost within the blur

of a moment moving out and making others.

Stroking your back through a nightmare

in the dark of your bedroom
I remember only
the panicked night
I woke your mother
and asked her to calm me,
hand to spine, not the many
times my parents
must have risen—half asleep,
their own dreams drifting—
and responded
likewise to my cries,
though their comfort
drifts inside the others
just as whatever twists in me
some way resides in you
and every palm sweeps up
a breath it presses
to our shoulder blades
and smooths.

Poems

They go like rabbits, is what I thought
and came and wrote down, though I know
nothing about rabbits. I knew poems before
they turned rabbit. The boy turned them rabbit,
his colic a spell. *Alakazam, alakazoodle,*
turn this brain into a noodle! Jon,
a month ago we were in your living room.
The boy was on your carpet eating fishy crackers
from a bowl. He was afraid of your cat
but still less afraid than of any other cat.
We had Nickelodeon on and we were talking
about Dad, about the Dad you knew before I was born
who was so busy while your mother was so sick
and how unerringly happy he managed to stay
through it all, as if he couldn't even *see* the darkness
let alone be swallowed by it. How you'd almost
forgiven him for that. And now all these tubes, Jon,
and nine bags of fluid syncopating through
your organs. I wanted to be Dad as badly as you.
The boy is in the waiting room. He likely
won't remember you, though I will tell him
story after story until a living room opens up
Alakazam inside him and in it a rabbit
eating fishy crackers on the carpet
while he sits in my chair beside you
talking provincial NDP and in another room
I kneel next to your mother's bed
as by the door you remove our father's hat
and hang it on its hook beside
his trench coat beaded with rainwater
which runs like rabbits (whatever rabbits are)
down the grey lawn and disappears.

King Tide

The boardwalks scuttled like diving-reef schooners—
a walkable Galilee if anyone dared, but each jogger rears
to higher ground. I've lost my son a half-second here
or there before I pulled him up, his lips like planks,
in tubs and pools and once a mirror lake—the obsidian,
endless kind that really ends abruptly in roots and husks
and carcasses and muck. This country's full of them.
All summer we swim bellies up, avoid anoxic thoughts.

The joggers, any other day, linger at the point
just long enough to catch their breath and contemplate
an app, perhaps the sun. *Yes, there it is, afloat.* My son,
I need to know what you thought of water when it first,
again, surrounded you. Your eyes were wide. You didn't
make a sound. Not one thing was born or died.

The Commons

–for E.D. Blodgett

No atom measures less than a man's hand
wrote a man whose hand turned flower.
You died the same November day as my brother,
so weeks passed before I learned
you'd lifted, black on grey, cawing
over the commons.

A friend I loved—I loved, at least, her letters—
one day weighed her head down in a stream.
A year of queries followed, then came
a coroner's report and her scattered
manuscripts. All birds, beautiful ones
I'd never seen.

Cape gannet, corncrake, rock kestrel,
weaverbird, river hawk, pink-backed
pelican.... No next of kin.
No will transferring rights.
Just bird after bird
into the night.

I remember your talk about Rumi:
the long empty walls of that room,
how you held us as his ghazals
held you. I remember words leaving
and others arriving, and between them
how bright the field.

Łazienki Park

I

At the moment, let's see,
seventeen cameras capturing
Chopin brooding beneath
his wind-amended willow tree.
To disappear is easier in Europe,
your language lost except
when held aloft by tour guides
who punctuate their talking points
by thrusting bright umbrellas.

My son, half-Polish, lounges
in his second sleep beside me,
language swirling in the cyclotron
behind his eyes. I haven't
spoken yet today. I may not.
I've removed my shoes in case
a warden of the park might think
I'm dusting up his fern-green bench.
Oh, rain! I'd say to him
if I knew the word for *rain*, or *oh*,
though I can guess the latter,
hear most every nation's version
as their tours convoy through the gate—
a moment's sound before a camera
obfuscates each face.

Geez, it's just a statue, just a man—
formidable, but still. But still each day
I bring my son to sit before the statue
in a place where, if Chopin could see,
he could see me, and feebly
and with great care, write, and hope
the words will sometime, somewhere,
blind to me and in a foreign tongue,
institute a sound not that unlike
the music all day raining
in Łazienki's entryway.

II

If the couple, age-incongruous, garbed,
respectively, in suit and cocktail dress,
are having an affair, it's going badly—
both so busy on their phones that even
Chopin on his perch is looking down
on them, while they absorb themselves
in something... god knows... anything...
other than the ornament they've entered.

III

Twigs, leaves, feathers, scum.
A neon tennis ball (hot pink and lime).
Drainage pipes, mood lights.
A mother and two pipping ducklings.
And water, of course: rifle green,
too shallow this summer night
for the flightless ducklings to climb out.
The mother flaps up, calls down from the edge
of Chopin's pissoir, paces below
the heeled shoes and billowed cloak
Szymanowski stuffed him in.

The infants guard their deaths nobly,
which is to say, in keeping with
their instincts. They circle and circle,
elude human meddling, tuned
only to their mother's calls,
which dwindle. I wheel my son out.
The park empties. Chopin's
tubercular head stays turned away,
his ear forever open to their song
and the following one.

IV

Chopin's right hand, behind him, reared up
like a mammal shot through with alarm.
No photo can capture both it and his measured face.
The tree above him a fist with too many fingers.

The tourist's hand wrenches the tripod, depresses
the timer, races to the small of his wife's back,
as in Old Town, the Ghetto, the Palace of Culture,
as in Krakow, Auschwitz, Gdansk, and the airport.

The nuns' faces obscured behind ice cream cones.
The garden blooming white and pink, luxuriating
beneath a massage of bees. The tension
in Chopin's absent hand. Everything recorded there.

V

NATO's in Warsaw, sweating Russia—
lame-duck Obama some blocks
from here, distracted, denouncing
shootings in America, by and of police.
No one ever gets away. Not really.
Not anymore.

A tour group, fifty-strong, rolls in—
a startled hedgehog spiked
with selfie-sticks. No one asks
for help, or company, and yet
each seems determined
to affix their face
in the middle of the scene.
Soon bored, they scroll their photos,
Facebook, news. Putin, the West,
the unfortunate election. Castile's car,
Sterling's parking lot, the hotel balcony
above the spot where an ambushed

Dallas officer was shot. Chopin,
the pond, the grass, the fevered trees.
Nothing's all that far.

And you? Oh hopeless, foolish, you.
There you are.

VI

One woman in the caravan
(pleated pants checkered
like a picnic blanket)
notices the bust of Liszt
tucked to the side, hurries
over with her iPad,
squares his face inside it,
fires. Her group already
loading back into the bus,
she turns and runs.

VII

No shadows, long or otherwise,
for the still-waking mind.
My son slopped in his stroller,
the early stirring in his throat
not yet arrived across the length of him.
Łazienki an encampment
for banded mallards
fixed with feathered spoilers,
flashing teal, filtering the swamps
sprinklers have strewn through
the gravel paths, mowing lawns
long before the groundsman
grumbles in. The benches
are empty. Not one runner yet.

Frédéric, look how the sun
administrates between the trees
to open, finally, your pond's
blue and cloudless eye.

summer night air
drifts through the dog-eared pages
of my father's Issa

On the Occasion of my Mother First Forgetting my Name

Volunteer babysitter in from the suburbs,
she kneels on our hardwood
towering blocks with her grandson.
In bed one room over, eyes open,
a rough night's lost sleep
as yet unrecovered, I hover.

Blocks clatter.
My son tests his new catchphrase:
"Oh no!"
"That's right, oh no!"
Her voice sieved through a smile.
My mother.

Oh you know who you are,
she'd said, her hand waving
the whole thing away
like her keys and credit cards,
the errands that
weren't worth the bother.

I place my palms
on my chest. I breathe.
The black ceiling tints grey.
Then comes the soft knock
of one block placed
on top of another.

The Baffled King

Silence, then shapes, then his voice
comes like a hand slowly, slowly
opening a door. *Washcloth,* we say
as we show him the washcloth.
Stingray, he says, trolling it through
bubbles. *Muffin,* he says, bunching it
into a cup. He puts a toy skateboard
on top of a doll. *Cowboy hat.*
He places one pumpkin seed
beside another. *Butterfly.*

Beside his crib I sing him a song
about pleasing the Lord. *Fire,* he'd said,
peeking into the bowl of popcorn. Then
together we'd placed it inside our mouths.
Through the cracked door I see my wife
in the kitchen pouring our tea, her hand
gripping the *elephant trunk.* I compose
and compose until he's wordless again
and I slip out, like every night, silent
and formless in the sudden light.

Diagnosis

Last night I dreamed I found you, Mom,
lost and wandering the city of my birth/your life—
I led you by the arm the long walk home.

I woke and in the dark beside my wife
(who tossed in dreams herself) wrote blindly,
panicked, the words palimpsesting,

interweaving limbs—trapped till morning
and the intricate forensics I'd enlist
to pry each character from each.

Worse the nightmare far but not apart
(I wrote, I think), whole universes linking
elbows in the night/night-thought

so that even now, so many hours after,
I can't confirm if it was my wife
who reached across and calmed me as I wrote

or you as we untangled, finally,
before your door, once also mine,
and all the winding corridors inside.

What did you dream about?

Wook, he answered, at one. One of his first words,
words coming to him slowly, so slowly, like shadows,
and less words than sounds, word-sounds
that did their work in mystery and in mystery
did better work than our common language
commonly could: *shapes* or *light* or *toys* or *love* or *nothing*—
"nothing" the common web search return.
He returns even now, at three, to his one answer,
one word—tradition-cemented but flowing inside.
Inside I know it will soon be replaced, this word,
by some sensible answer, some shadow's shadow
his mind's stitched together. We're together each morning;
I'm ready, but his answer remains. He'll remain
the boy after the answer, the answer remaining
after the boy and his dreams. The dreams gone,
all too common, the word stripped of all but the sound,
the mystery given and given to me, a shadow for my shadow.
What does it mean? I repeat. He repeats it, gives me a look.
Wook is the answer; the answer I'm seeking is *wook*.

Most days you still remember

the December when Dad died
and the sewer lines froze up
and overflowed. You remember
that the man you loved
before you met my father
crashed into a hydro pole
but forget the future you'd expected
before answering the phone.

I wrote once about that first night
I dressed to pee at two a.m. (winter boots
and jacket over PJs) and made my way
across the street, the neighbour's
key tight in my palm, and how
that simple trip alone transformed me—
the darkness crisp and endless
overhead and in each step
I punctured through the snow.

Now I think instead about our neighbour
waking slightly to her creaking door
then remembering enough
to roll back toward her dream
which mattered then—the warmth
of its returning—while I fumbled
for the bathroom light and some other boy
in some forgotten future
woke and called your name.

Old Game

The face comes last, a blank canvas,
like a tulip snowballed long inside the bulb
as the body roots down-wire.
The prize for wins a mutilated corpse.

Each time, my son insists I pen him in—
his limbs, his face (the Xed-out eyes,
drooped lips and dangled tongue).
Loss and victory the same.

There, I say, *he's dead, okay?* He grins.
Then my child lets me set the gallows,
blank some vital word, and list again
the alphabet from which all this is made.

Why and Why

The coyote was in the field before we arrived
sunning itself in the sprung grass
only rose to its haunches
after we'd entered the clearing
my mother, my son, their vocabulary
a passed baton so now he reminds her
river Grammy the word is river
field Grammy field until he's raced
ahead of us into it further and further
and finally I spot the coyote there
in the green rising and I run
my mother forgotten behind me
I run as the coyote readies
and I snatch my son up and away
remembering, gathering both of them close
offering the word *coyote*
neither understanding why and why
we're backing through the forest toward
the trailhead, the morning, the night
when the coyote stepped silently
out of one field and into the next.

Transmission Tower

A bee flaps its four wings 230 times per second
to make a sound we vent through teeth.

Our tireless machines pull power from a river, run it down
the ribbons that turn my son, beneath, to tuning fork.

He's three. I place one finger to his ear tip—*pinna,*
Latin word for auricle and wing—and that hive sings.

He calls out in the night, sometimes, for my hand
to glide across the oxbow water of his back.

Still half asleep I count the strokes, the years until
he's lived as long as I did with a father.

His mouth, his eyes, alive when he first sensed the sound—
electricity inside he couldn't hear without my hand.

Then my turn, his finger on my ear.
A thousand tiny thrusts of air.

Reprieve

It's like a dream, the doctor says.
He claps my mother's back and ticks
the boxes for more meds. One blister pack
each day and my mother stays, for now,
the same or better. Again she knows my name,
each place we've lived, what my father did
before he died. When she hugs me now,
chin-high, she remembers once again
the shape and how, when I was small,
her spot was mine. She reaches back sometimes.
Her question comes to me as if across
our long-discarded dinner table. I say I'm fine.
I ask about her pills. *It's like a dream,*
she says. I nod. The moment passes by.

Return to Roblin

we crashed awake, frantic
at almost sleeping through
what we would come to realize was
your lifetime of last breaths

                        —Elizabeth Ross

I stand beside the frozen millpond,
my breath
rising over my face.

I come now for the place, not for you,
which was your point.
The land never stops turning up.

My son, whose first crawl sent him
sidewise under your wife's wingback,
now chants the continents in mnemonic song:

Tell me the continents,
tell me the continents,
tell me if you can.

"This is what Antarctica looks like,"
I'll say when I show him
my photos.

The snapping turtles another
houseguest wrote of, years ago now,
swim slowly under the ice.

When I tell my son this
neither of us will really believe it.
Three years have passed.

My student who died in her sleep
would have graduated by now—
would have left me in the usual way.

Your gravestone's in good shape.
The turtle figurine remains there,
huddled in snow.

Antarctica is crumbling,
whole Manhattans
falling off.

They are like cities underwater
and the undulating green waves of time
are laid on them.

"But how do they breathe?" my son will ask
and through the green waves
I will venture to answer.

Are your flies grass, like mine?

Last time, I think,
I'll brush the flies
from my father's face.

                    —Kobayashi Issa

You show me a photo of your wedding party
and name nearly all but the since-divorced spouses,
yet still I wake at four a.m. and scrawl
Are your flies grass, like mine?,
though flies these days are photographs
papering the dying and the dead.

Dad is almost all photo now
and cassette recording, tapes stretched
and slurred and sputtering near-transparent:
sermons and, once, his voice guiding me
through an Early Reader—me insisting
the "g" in "laughed" is hard, him lagging
and lagging until I lagged, too.
Or was that voice you? Twenty-five years
I've had you carry him inside.

Mom, I'm sick with flies and grass
and photographs. When I gasp at four a.m.
I need you out there gasping, too—
the name of yet another great aunt
rescued, written down,
to be recited (finger dusting face)
to your lagging son that afternoon.

Matryoshka

I asked of everything
if it had
something more

—Pablo Neruda

My father, my brothers, my mother, our son,
then you, love, and lastly always the rabbit,
silver-eyed and dun. I line them up.
Put them back one in the next. Nothing
inside the rabbit, only the rabbit in you,
our son always surrounding, surrounded.
Nothing will change but I start again.
They screech at their joints as they part—
my father, my brothers, my mother, our son.
Their paint fades. I bring them together.
My father's face worn to nothing. I pull them apart.
My brothers' suits, my mother's nightgown,
our son's wide open mouth. All the same.
I pull them together. I bring them apart.
There you are, your hair wild, holding
everything up. The rabbit you carry untouched.

Now I must be gentle

Now I must be gentle
when I wake
if the moment allows
(it never allows).

I must barely ruffle
the gauze—
maybe light outside
maybe not yet.

Do you set out
when I first turn for bed
or before
or not until
just when I stir?

Are you waiting
and watching together?

It took me so long
to gather your message
to stop gathering—

to be gentle
if the moment allows.

Long Distance

We all sound houndy on the phone,
too low, too old. We all have colds.
So son when you moan for Elmo
below your mother's voice,
your vowels long slow animals
growling the miles, you are not
three, or you, or quite another.
You're something new:
my father's laughter echoed
back through convoluted
tubes, or a siren for some
unremorseful danger,
or my body sunk in water
till I hear, eventually, my heart
outside arriving as a stranger.

Notes

The epigraph on the book's dedication page is from the poem "LaHave River, Cable Ferry" by Chris Banks (*The Cold Panes of Surfaces,* Nightwood Editions, 2006).

The book's epigraph is from the novel *For Whom the Bell Tolls* by Ernest Hemingway (Scribner, 1940).

"Strangers" is dedicated to Elise Partridge.

The title "Smoothing the Holy Surfaces" is taken from Pablo Neruda's "Ode to Ironing." The translation is as it appears in the epigraph to P.K. Page's glosa "Planet Earth" (*Planet Earth: Poems Selected and New,* The Porcupine's Quill, 2002). I have yet to find the same translation elsewhere.

"Weather in Dublin" includes slightly modified lines from Seamus Heaney's poems "Bogland" and "Digging." The originals are "The wet centre is bottomless" and "Under my window, a clean rasping sound" (*Opened Ground: Selected Poems 1966-1996,* Farrar, Straus and Giroux, 1998).

The italicized lines in "Ultrasound" are from "Sonnet 2:29" by Rainer Maria Rilke, as translated under the title "Being" by Don Paterson (*Orpheus,* Faber, 2006).

The poem that inspired "The Future" was "The Dead" by Sue Sinclair (*Heaven's Thieves,* Brick Books, 2016).

The Mary Oliver epigraph to "What Wisdom's in Wisdom Recorded?" is from her essay "Of Power and Time" (*Upstream,* Penguin Press, 2016).

I wrote "At Roblin Lake" while Writer-in-Residence at the Al Purdy A-frame. The sequence draws from a great number of Al Purdy's poems, most notably "Arctic Rhododendrons," "The Country North of Belleville," "The Dead Poet," "In Search of Owen Roblin," "In the Early Cretaceous," "Inside the Mill," "Interruption," "Piling Blood" and "Untitled." "At Roblin Lake" is dedicated to Eurithe Purdy.

The Al Purdy epigraph to "As the Dream Holds the Real" is from his poem "Inside the Mill" (*Beyond Remembering*, Harbour Publishing, 2000).

The Robbie Burns epigraph to "Interruption" is from his poem "To a Mouse."

The Louise Glück epigraph to "Last Embers" is from her poem "Burning Leaves" (*A Village Life*, Farrar, Strauss and Giroux, 2010). The italicized lines are from Al Purdy's poem "The Country North of Belleville" (*Beyond Remembering*).

The Jim Harrison epigraph to "Voices" is from his poem "Debtors" (*Songs of Unreason*, Copper Canyon Press, 2011). "Voices" is dedicated to Jim Taylor, Jr.

The Wallace Stevens epigraph to "The Artist" is from his poem "Of Mere Being" (*Wallace Stevens: Poems Selected by John Burnside*, Faber and Faber, 2008).

"Poems" is dedicated to Jon Taylor.

The opening line of "The Commons" is from "Ms Cassie & Apollo" by Richard Outram (*The Essential Richard Outram*, The Porcupine's Quill, 2011). The original version includes a line break between "than" and "a." In addition to E.D. Blodgett, "The Commons" is also dedicated to L.S. Mensah.

The Kobayashi Issa epigraph to "Are you flies grass, like mine?" is a haiku presented in full, as translated by Robert Hass (*The Essential Haiku: Versions of Basho, Buson, and Issa*, Ecco, 1994). Much thanks to Helen Gowans for a conversation that sparked this poem.

The Elizabeth Ross epigraph to "Return to Roblin" is from her poem "Afterbirth" (*After Birth*, Palimpsest Press, 2019). The italicized lines near the end of the poem are from Al Purdy's poem "The Country North of Belleville." The poem by the other "houseguest" is Nick Thran's "Poem With Too Many Turtles"

(*Mayor Snow,* Nightwood Editions, 2015).

The Pablo Neruda epigraph to "Matryoshka" is from his poem "Investigations," as translated by Alastair Reid (*Fully Empowered,* Farrar, Strauss and Giroux, 2001).

Acknowledgments

Poems in this book have been published previously in *The Cascadia Review, The Fiddlehead, Frogpond, HALIBUT, Juniper, long con magazine, The Malahat Review, The New Quarterly, Train: a poetry journal, Vallum, Watch Your Head* and the anthology *Sweet Water: Poems for the Watersheds* (Caitlin Press, 2020).

"You ask me about my mother," "Smoothing the Holy Surfaces," "That Scar," "Lunch," and "A Normal Day" were published as the chapbook *Smoothing the Holy Surfaces* by The Alfred Gustav Press in 2012. "Łazienki Park" was published as a chapbook of the same name by The Alfred Gustav Press in 2017. "At Roblin Lake" and "Return to Roblin" (as "Tell Me If You Can") were published in the chapbook *The Green Waves: Poems from Roblin Lake* by 845 Press in 2019.

Thank you to the editors and publishers of each.

—

Much of this book was written on the shared traditional territories of the kʷikʷəƛ̓əm (Kwikwetlem), xʷməθkʷəy̓əm (Musqueam), Sḵwx̱wú7mesh Úxwumixw (Squamish) and səl̓ilwətaʔɬ (Tsleil-Waututh) peoples.

Thank you to the O'Melinn and Swanson families for the time they granted me over the years to write in their cabins. Thank you, similarly, to the Kidd family, and to Ann and Martin Sheriff, for the opportunities they gave me to write in (blessed!) isolation.

Thank you to Eurithe Purdy, Jean Baird and the Al Purdy A-frame Association for the chance to work in Al and Eurithe's place. I can think of no finer gift for a writer.

Thank you to the Canada Council for the Arts, for the grant they gave me so many years ago they probably decided the book would never come (I thought so, too, at times).

Thank you to Raoul Fernandes, Nora Gould, Elena Johnson, Bren Simmers, Karen Solie, Kevin Spenst, Rhea Tregebov, and my UBC classmates for editorial notes on some of these poems.

Thank you to my editor, Luke Hathaway, for believing in me and in this book, and for helping me see what both could be. Thank you to Dan, Vanessa, Christina and everyone else at Biblioasis for giving the book its best possible home.

Thank you to strangers made friends. And strange friends. And family. I lost too many people I love dearly during the writing of this book. I've tried, futile as it is, to hold you all here.

To Grace. To Lucas. To Marta.

To you, Mom.

Author photo: Marta Taylor

Rob Taylor is the author of four poetry collections, including *The News* (Gaspereau Press, 2016), which was a finalist for the Dorothy Livesay Poetry Prize. He is also the editor of *What the Poets Are Doing: Canadian Poets in Conversation* (Nightwood Editions, 2018) and guest editor of *Best Canadian Poetry 2019* (Biblioasis, 2019). He lives in Port Moody, BC, with his wife and children.